MOVIES from Then to Now

BY RACHEL GRACK

SEQUENCE

AMICUS | AMICUS INK

Sequence is published by Amicus and Amicus Ink
P.O. Box 227, Mankato, MN 56002
www.amicuspublishing.us

Library of Congress Cataloging-in-Publication Data
Names: Koestler-Grack, Rachel A., 1973- author.
Title: Movies from then to now / Rachel A. Koestler-Grack.
Description: Mankato : Amicus, 2022. | Series: Sequence. Developments in technology | Includes bibliographical references and index. | Audience: Ages 7-10 | Audience: Grades 2-3 | Summary: "Full-color photographs and a running timeline illustrate important developments in film and movie history for elementary readers. Topics feature the invention of photography, Thomas Edison's kinetograph camera, silent film evolution to sound and color, 3-D movies, IMAX theaters, digital video, and virtual reality. A table of contents, glossary, further resources, and an index are included"-- Provided by publisher.
Identifiers: LCCN 2019037096 (print) | LCCN 2019037097 (ebook) | ISBN 9781681519616 (library binding) | ISBN 9781681526089 (paperback) | ISBN 9781645490463 (pdf)
Subjects: LCSH: Motion pictures--History--Juvenile literature.
Classification: LCC PN1993.5.A1 K644 2022 (print) | LCC PN1993.5.A1 (ebook) | DDC 791.4309--dc23
LC record available at https://lccn.loc.gov/2019037096
LC ebook record available at https://lccn.loc.gov/2019037097

Editor: Gillia Olson
Designer: Aubrey Harper
Photo Researcher: Bridget Prehn

Photo Credits: Age Fotostock/JT Vintage 11; Alamy 15, 26–27, Allstar Picture Library 27 (inset), Foto Arena LTDA 4, Pictorial Press Ltd 7 (inset), 20, Science History Images 8–9, Sportsphoto 24; AP/Bei piao/Imaginechina 28–29; Denver Museum of Nature & Science/ Rick Wicker 22–23; Flickr/Gordon Werner 18–19; Getty/Science & Society Picture Library 12; Heritage Auctions/HA.com 16 (both); iStock/Andrey_Kuzmin cover (seats), BlackJack3D cover (background film), DNY59 cover (curtain), KOHb circuit background (throughout), PhonlamaiPhoto cover (camera), SKrow cover (projector), iStock/YvanDube 21; Shutterstock/ Everett Historical 6–7, Who is Danny cover (background); Wikimedia/Marcellin Auzolle 12 (inset), PD56 15 (inset)

TABLE OF CONTENTS

William George Horner invents the first zoetrope.

1834

. . L O A D I N G . . . L O A D I N G

The First Motion Pictures

How many movies do you watch every week? Think about life before movies. People went to plays with real actors on stage. People listened to live music. At home, children played with toys. In 1834, William George Horner invented a **zoetrope**. Its spinning artwork seemed to move. His toy inspired the idea of movies.

When a person spins a zoetrope and looks through the slot, the pictures seem to move.

ADING . . . LOADING . . . LOADING . . .

Photography was invented in 1839. To make a movie, you need many pictures taken very fast. Early cameras were too slow. In 1877, Eadweard Muybridge lined up 12 cameras beside a racetrack. Each one took a picture as a horse ran past. He put the photos in a zoetrope. He created the first motion picture.

Muybridge's horse pictures became the first motion picture.

William George Horner invents the first zoetrope.

1834

1877

Eadweard Muybridge creates the first motion picture.

Eadweard Muybridge

ADING . . . LOADING . . . LOADING . . .

William George Horner invents the first zoetrope.

Émile Reynaud invents the Optical Theater.

1834

1877

1888

G . . . LOADING

Eadweard Muybridge creates the first motion picture.

Meanwhile, Émile Reynaud was trying to show moving drawings on a screen. He experimented with his toy—the Praxinoscope. Using light and mirrors, he could **project** his drawings. In 1888, he designed the Optical Theater. This machine projected hand-colored **film** instead of paper pictures. His movies became the first cartoons.

Reynaud played his Optical Theater cartoons for crowds in France.

Movies of real people still needed a new camera. In 1891, Thomas Edison's company invented the Kinetograph. It took pictures at 40 frames per second. The camera used strips of plastic film called **celluloid**. This film is still used today. Edison put the Kinetograph camera into the Kinetoscope. This device let one person at a time watch a short movie.

To watch a Kinetoscope movie, a person looked through a small hole while film moved past.

1834	William George Horner invents the first zoetrope.
1877	Eadweard Muybridge creates the first motion picture.
1888	Émile Reynaud invents the Optical Theater.
1891	Thomas Edison's company invents the first motion picture camera.

LOADING

ADING . . . LOADING . . . LOADING . . .

1834 — William George Horner invents the first zoetrope.

1877 — Eadweard Muybridge creates the first motion picture.

1888 — Émile Reynaud invents the Optical Theater.

1891 — Thomas Edison's company invents the first motion picture camera.

1894 — Auguste and Louis Lumiére invent the cinématographe.

Inventors soon found a way to play films for crowds. In 1894, Auguste and Louis Lumiére built the cinématographe. Its projector moved at only 16 frames per second, but that was fast enough to show movement. It was also much smaller and lighter than the Kinetograph. Films played on-screen became known as the **cinema**.

The cinématographe projector cast the movie on-screen, as shown in an ad for one of the shows (inset).

ADING . . . LOADING . . . LOADING . . .

Loud, Colorful, and in Your Face

Most early movies were silent. Some theaters played records. It was hard to get sound to match up with the picture. In 1927, Warner Brothers tried new equipment in its theaters. The sound and picture matched. In 1928, they released *The Jazz Singer*. Actors talked! People loved it. They started calling these movies "talkies."

Eugenie Besserer and Al Jolson acted in *The Jazz Singer*, the first successful "talkie."

1834	William George Horner invents the first zoetrope.
1877	Eadweard Muybridge creates the first motion picture.
1888	Émile Reynaud invents the Optical Theater.
1891	Thomas Edison's company invents the first motion picture camera.
1894	Auguste and Louis Lumiére invent the cinématographe.
1928	*The Jazz Singer* matches up sound and pictures, introducing "talkies."

ADING . . . LOADING . . . LOADING . . .

1834: William George Horner invents the first zoetrope.

1877: Eadweard Muybridge creates the first motion picture.

1888: Émile Reynaud invents the Optical Theater.

1891: Thomas Edison's company invents the first motion picture camera.

1894: Auguste and Louis Lumiére invent the cinématographe.

1928: *The Jazz Singer* matches up sound and pictures, introducing "talkies."

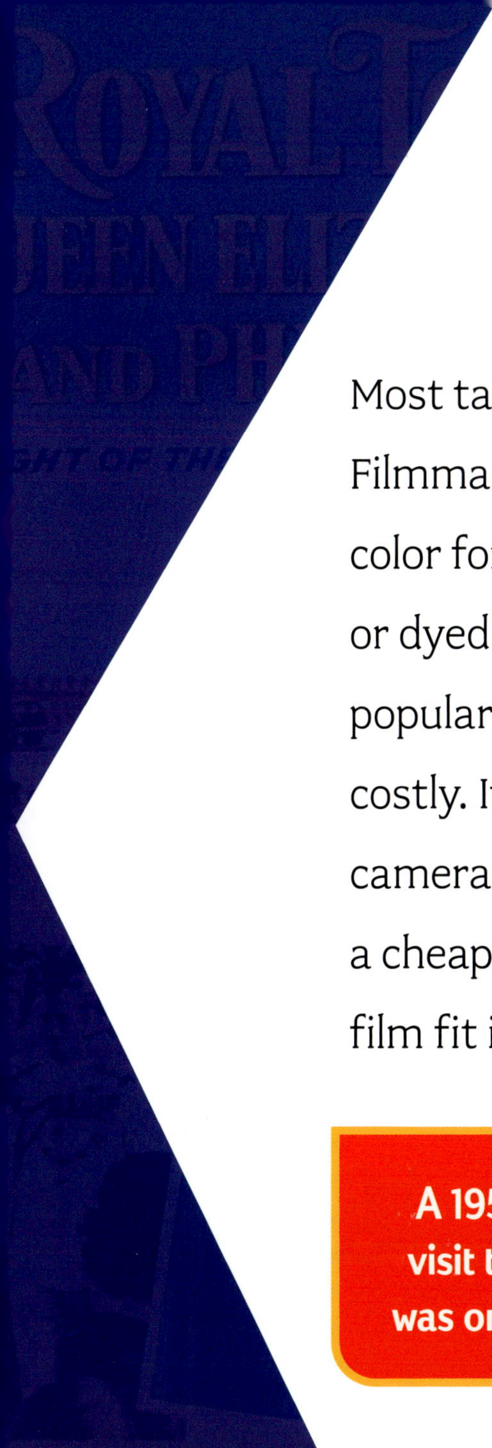

Most talkies were black-and-white. Filmmakers had experimented with color for years. Some hand-colored or dyed the film. Technicolor became popular in the 1930s. The film was costly. It also used a special kind of camera. In 1950, Eastman color made a cheaper way. Its single-layer color film fit into any movie camera.

A 1951 movie of Queen Elizabeth's visit to Canada, *The Royal Journey*, was one of the first in Eastman color.

1950

LOADING... LOADING...

Eastman color film makes color movies common.

By 1950, many people owned televisions. Moviemakers had to find new ways to wow viewers. In 1952, Cinerama tried a widescreen. It took three cameras and three projectors to show a movie. The big screen curved around audiences. It drew them into the action. These screens inspired the ones used in theaters today.

Cinerama used three projectors and seven speakers to make the audience feel inside the movie.

- 1834 — William George Horner invents the first zoetrope.
- 1877 — Eadweard Muybridge creates the first motion picture.
- 1888 — Émile Reynaud invents the Optical Theater.
- 1891 — Thomas Edison's company invents the first motion picture camera.
- 1894 — Auguste and Louis Lumiére invent the cinématographe.
- 1928 — *The Jazz Singer* matches up sound and pictures, introducing "talkies."

Cinerama offers widescreen movies.

1950 1952 ING . . . LOADING . . .

Eastman color film makes color movies common.

Audience members wear their 3-D glasses to a movie in the 1950s.

- **1834** William George Horner invents the first zoetrope.
- **1877** Eadweard Muybridge creates the first motion picture.
- **1888** Émile Reynaud invents the Optical Theater.
- **1891** Thomas Edison's company invents the first motion picture camera.
- **1894** Auguste and Louis Lumiére invent the cinématographe.
- **1928** *The Jazz Singer* matches up sound and pictures, introducing "talkies."

What if the action popped right out of the screen? In 1953, *House of Wax* became the first major **3-D** movie. These movies play using two cameras. One serves as the right eye. The other camera is the left. Their pictures overlap on-screen. Special 3-D glasses separate them to create shape. People and objects appear to pop out of the screen.

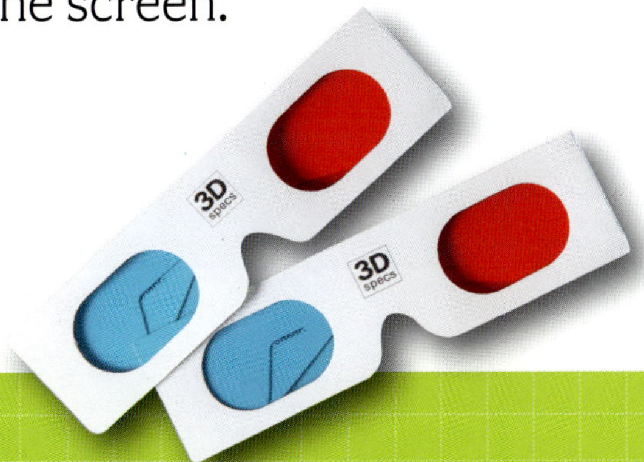

1950 – Eastman color film makes color movies common.

1952 – Cinerama offers widescreen movies.

1953 – *House of Wax* is the first major 3-D movie.

. . . LOADING . . .

In 1971, the first IMAX theater opened in Toronto, Canada. IMAX screens curve around the viewer. People feel like they are almost in the movie. Some people even get **motion sickness**. IMAX screens can be huge. The biggest is as tall as a seven-story building. IMAX uses the largest film format in history. It's 10 times the size of regular movies.

IMAX theaters today also show 3-D movies.

1834 — William George Horner invents the first zoetrope.

1877 — Eadweard Muybridge creates the first motion picture.

1888 — Émile Reynaud invents the Optical Theater.

1891 — Thomas Edison's company invents the first motion picture camera.

1894 — Auguste and Louis Lumiére invent the cinématographe.

1928 — *The Jazz Singer* matches up sound and pictures, introducing "talkies."

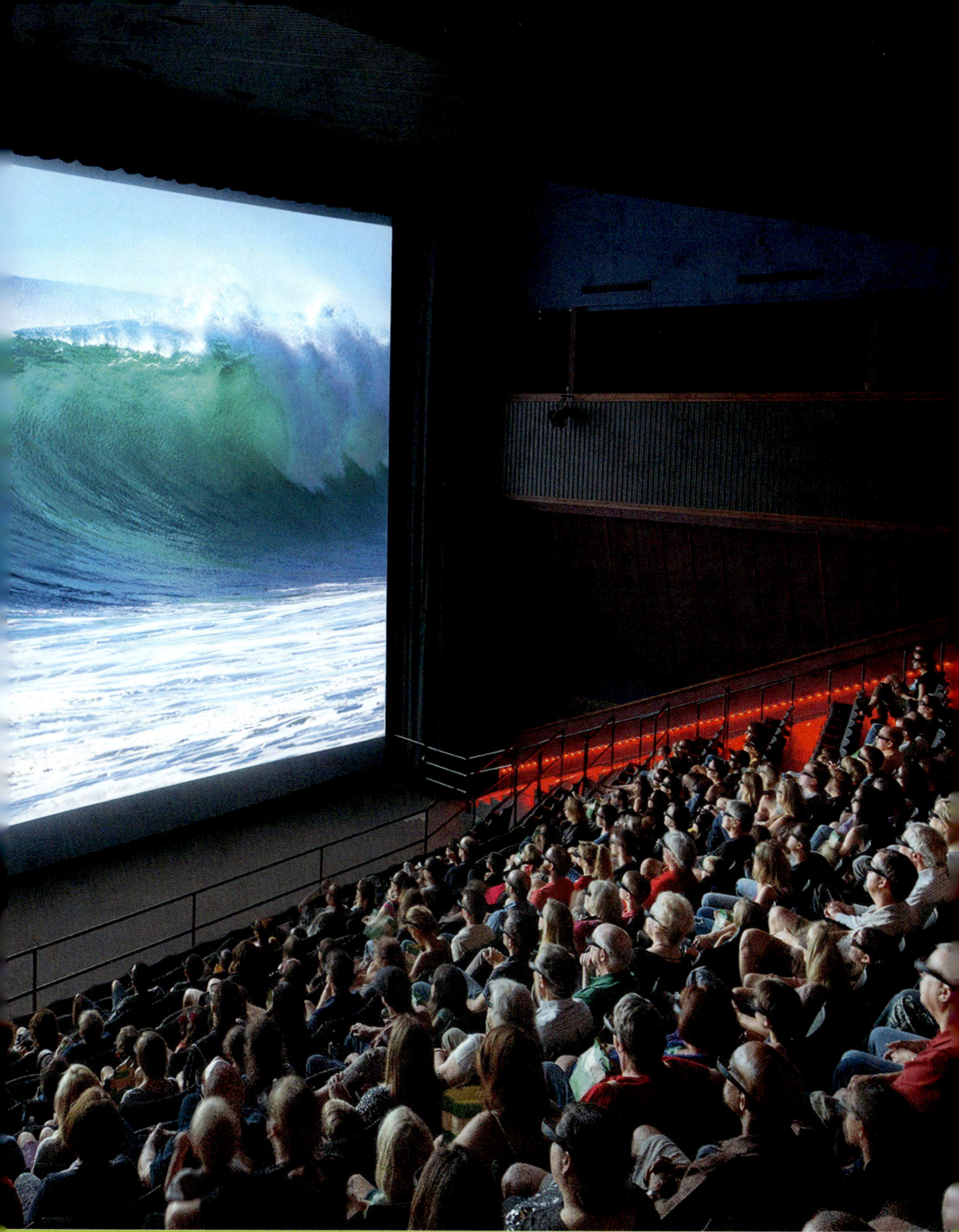

Cinerama offers widescreen movies.

The first IMAX theater opens in Toronto, Canada.

1950 1952 1953 1971

ADING . . .

Eastman color film makes color movies common.

House of Wax is the first major 3-D movie.

- **1834** William George Horner invents the first zoetrope.
- **1877** Eadweard Muybridge creates the first motion picture.
- **1888** Émile Reynaud invents the Optical Theater.
- **1891** Thomas Edison's company invents the first motion picture camera.
- **1894** Auguste and Louis Lumiére invent the cinématographe.
- **1928** *The Jazz Singer* matches up sound and pictures, introducing "talkies."

Movies by Computer

Computers began to help with movie **special effects** in 1973. Pictures and settings could be added digitally. An actor could look like he was fighting a real alien—on Mars! But could a whole movie be made by computer? Pixar thought so. In 1995, Disney and Pixar presented *Toy Story*. It was the first fully computer-animated movie.

Disney / Pixar's *Toy Story* was the first movie made fully by computer animation.

1950	Eastman color film makes color movies common.
1952	Cinerama offers widescreen movies.
1953	*House of Wax* is the first major 3-D movie.
1971	The first IMAX theater opens in Toronto, Canada.
1995	Pixar creates the first fully computer-animated movie.

By 2000, moviemakers were trying digital video. George Lucas filmed *Star Wars: Episode II* in digital. Digital cameras record pictures on computer chips instead of film. It's much cheaper. Copies last longer, too. In 2014, Paramount Pictures decided to use only digital video. It was the first movie company to do so.

***Star Wars: Episode II* was one of the first movies filmed all in digital.**

- **1834** William George Horner invents the first zoetrope.
- **1877** Eadweard Muybridge creates the first motion picture.
- **1888** Émile Reynaud invents the Optical Theater.
- **1891** Thomas Edison's company invents the first motion picture camera.
- **1894** Auguste and Louis Lumiére invent the cinématographe.
- **1928** *The Jazz Singer* matches up sound and pictures, introducing "talkies."

- 1950: Eastman color film makes color movies common.
- 1952: Cinerama offers widescreen movies.
- 1953: *House of Wax* is the first major 3-D movie.
- 1971: The first IMAX theater opens in Toronto, Canada.
- 1995: Pixar creates the first fully computer-animated movie.
- 2014: **Paramount Pictures offers only digital video.**

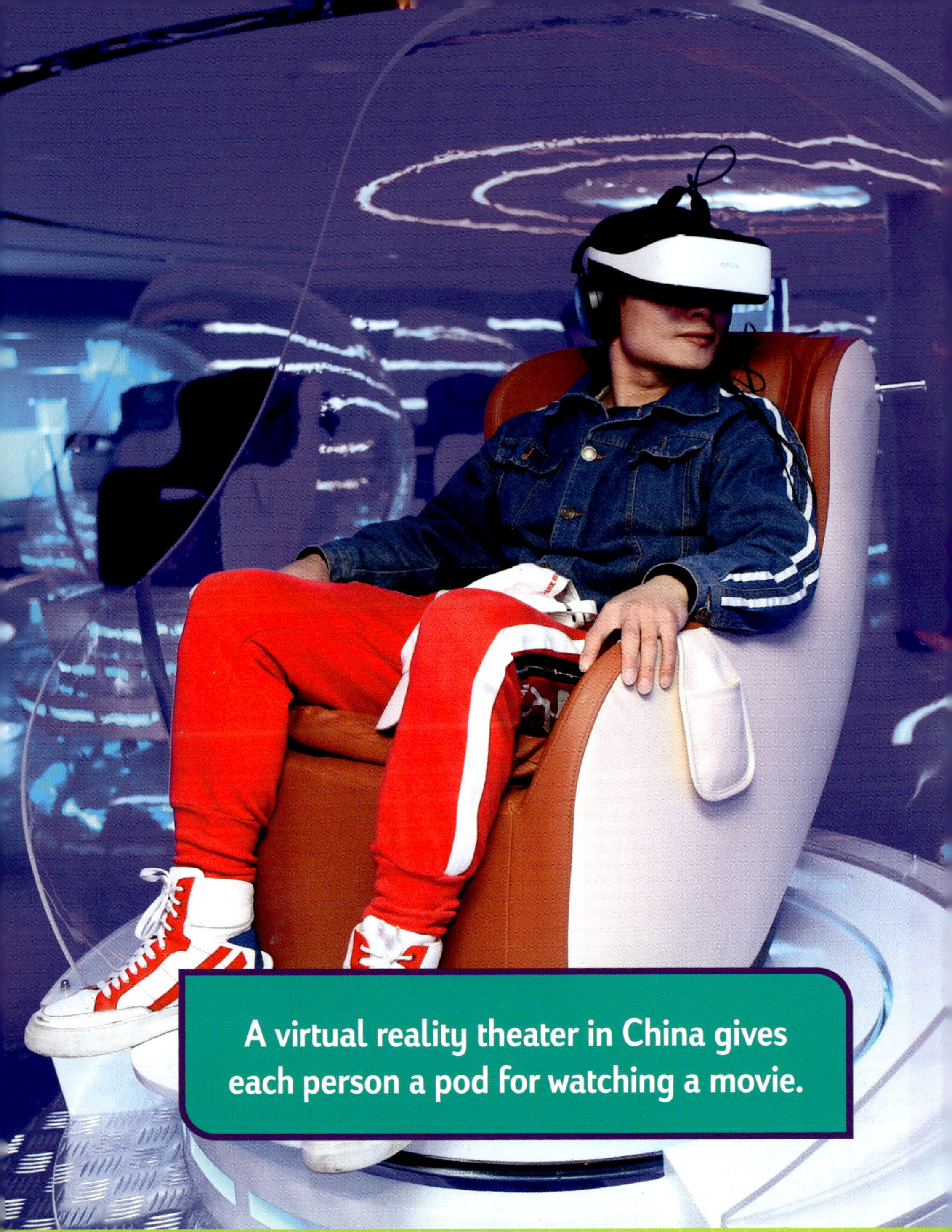

A virtual reality theater in China gives each person a pod for watching a movie.

- 1834 — William George Horner invents the first zoetrope.
- 1877 — Eadweard Muybridge creates the first motion picture.
- 1888 — Émile Reynaud invents the Optical Theater.
- 1891 — Thomas Edison's company invents the first motion picture camera.
- 1894 — Auguste and Louis Lumiére invent the cinématographe.
- 1928 — *The Jazz Singer* matches up sound and pictures, introducing "talkies."

Into the Future!

Today, many people **stream** movies on tablets or cellphones. Theaters are looking for ways to keep customers. Theaters are experimenting with **virtual reality** (VR). VR headsets put you right in the middle of the action. You interact with your virtual surroundings. Someday, you might star in your own movie!

1950 Eastman color film makes color movies common.

1952 Cinerama offers widescreen movies.

1953 *House of Wax* is the first major 3-D movie.

1971 The first IMAX theater opens in Toronto, Canada.

1995 Pixar creates the first fully computer-animated movie.

2014 Paramount Pictures offers only digital video.

Glossary

celluloid A tough, plastic strip of film used to make movies.

cinema Movies played on-screen; cinema can also be a theater.

digital video Video recorded using computers or other electronics.

film A roll of plastic strip used to take photographs; also, to record a motion picture; also, another name for a movie.

motion sickness Illness caused by movement or feeling of movement.

project To show an image on a screen.

special effects Things added to movies that can't be done by normal means, such as creating dinosaurs or traveling to another planet.

stream To move data in a steady flow, as in video or audio from a website to a computer or phone.

talkies A nickname for early movies with sound and voices.

3-D Having a feeling of depth within a flat picture; 3-D stands for "three-dimensional."

virtual reality A place created by computers that is not real but makes you feel like you are inside it; virtual reality is often viewed through headsets over your eyes.

zoetrope A toy that has drawings on the inside of a drum and slits for viewing on the outside; when the drum is turned, the drawings look like moving pictures.

Read More

Colby, Jennifer. *Silent Films to 3D Movies.* 21st Century Library: Then to Now Tech. Ann Arbor, Mich.: Cherry Lake Publishing, 2019.

Higgins, Nadia. *Making a Movie.* Sequence: Entertainment. Mankato, Minn.: Amicus/Amicus Ink, 2019.

Kenney, Karen Latchana. *Who Invented the Movie Camera?: Edison vs. Friese-Greene.* Alternator Books: STEM Smackdown. Minneapolis, Minn.: Lerner Publications, 2018.

Websites

Britannica: History of the Motion Picture: Media

www.britannica.com/art/history-of-the-motion-picture/images-videos

Pixar's Zoetrope and How Animation Works

https://thekidshouldseethis.com/post/17452504790

Ted ED: A Journey Through Visual Effects

https://ed.ted.com/lessons/a-cinematic-journey-through-visual-effects-don-levy

Index

About the Author

Rachel Grack has worked in children's nonfiction publishing since 1999. Rachel lives on a small desert ranch in Arizona. She enjoys spending time with her family and barnyard of animals. Thanks to our wireless world, her ranch stays tapped into developing technology.